TIME TRAVEL MAZES

Andy Peters

ARCTURUS

This edition published in 2014 by Arcturus Publishing Limited
26/27 Bickels Yard, 151–153 Bermondsey Street,
London SE1 3HA

ISBN: 978-1-78212-985-1
CH004028NT
Supplier 26, Date 0514, Print run 3142

Illustrations and mazes designed by Andy Peters
Written by Joe Fullman
Edited by Kate Overy
Designed by Tokiko Morishima

Printed in China

CONTENTS

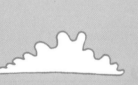

Chapter 1
A Magic Machine

It's the school holidays and Max, Millie, and Mojo are visiting a museum. Mojo wants to see the dinosaur bones first! But little do they know that their fun day out will soon turn into an amazing adventure through time!

Look out for Ted the ginger cat. He's tagged along and pops up in every maze!

Museum Muddle

Guide the gang through the giant dinosaur fossils. Max would love to see a real dinosaur. You never know, his wish might just come true!

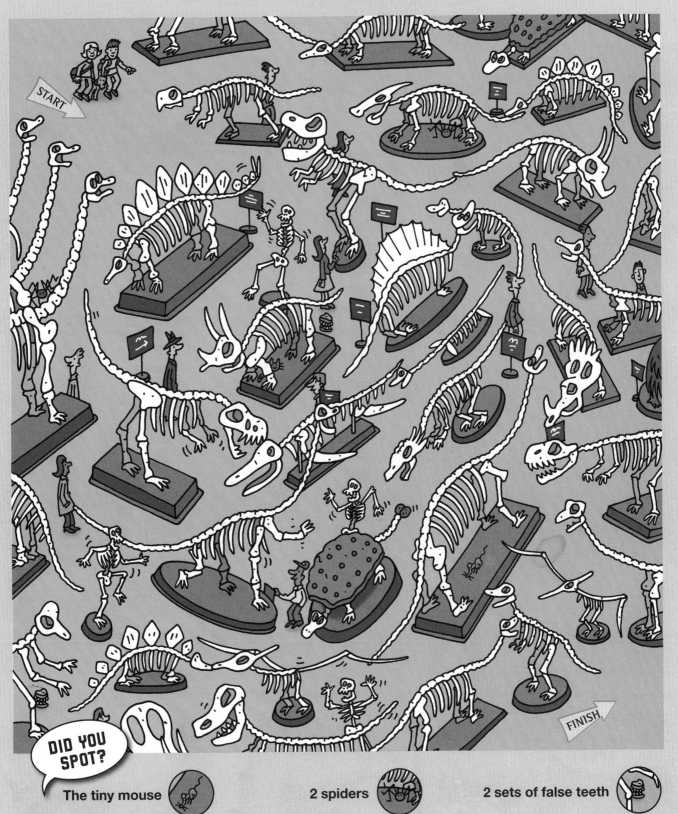

DID YOU SPOT?

The tiny mouse   2 spiders   2 sets of false teeth

Medieval Madness!

They'll have to be careful making their way through this collection of scary medieval exhibits. It's full of sharp swords, axes, and daggers.

DID YOU SPOT?

3 dropped gauntlets   The horse anklet   2 jewel-encrusted swords

Travels Through Time

It's a room filled with amazing machines from the past. But what's that mysterious box in the next room? Help the gang find a path through to it.

DID YOU SPOT?

The dropped helmet   The alien   3 dropped coffee cups

7

Today

The Time Machine

As they stand in front of the box, it suddenly opens to reveal something quite extraordinary – a real-life time machine! The gang can't wait to have a look.

The instruction manual

3 mice

Today

Taking Control!

Max, Millie, and Mojo are sitting in the time machine, trying to work out how to make it go. It's very complicated! Can you find the way through the controls to the 'on' switch?

DID YOU SPOT?

The missing screwdriver

3 dropped pencils

Time Tumble

Oh no! The time machine has taken off and Max and Millie are now whizzing through time.
But Mojo has been thrown clear of the craft. Help him get back to the others.

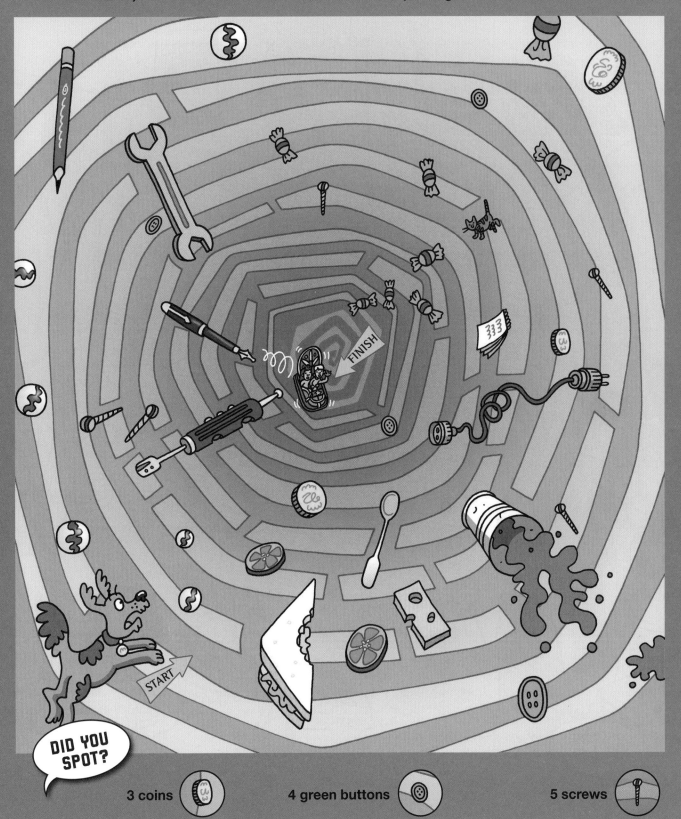

DID YOU SPOT?

3 coins   4 green buttons   5 screws

Crash Landing

What a strange place! The time machine has crash landed thousands of years in the future.
It seems to be broken. What will they do? Perhaps there's someone in that big palace who can fix it.

START

FINISH

DID YOU SPOT?

The hoverboard   2 flying cars   6 robots

Future Fix

The leader of the future city may look scary, but she's really very nice and is happy to help the gang. Guide them through the palace workshop to where the robots are fixing their craft.

DID YOU SPOT?

The dropped spanner　　　2 robot dogs　　　4 sonic screwdrivers

11

Chapter 2
Monster Mayhem

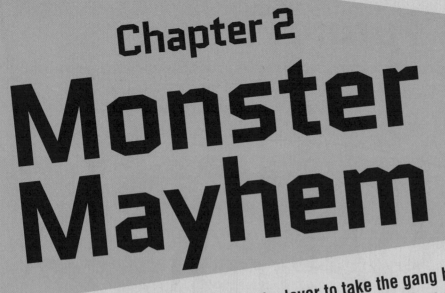

The time machine is working again, but the lever to take the gang back to the present is broken. That means they must either go into the future or into the past. They decide to head back to the past. Maybe they can find someone to fix the controls – and have a few adventures on the way!

Ferny Forest

Max and Millie set the controls for 'long ago' and have landed in a hot, steamy forest. Where and when are they? Time to do some exploring. Help them through the ferns to the jungle clearing.

70 million years ago

DID YOU SPOT?

The bird's nest

3 bumble bees

3 blue feathers

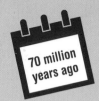

Grazing Giants

The clearing is full of huge dinosaurs eating their lunch! Guide Max, Millie, and Mojo between all the munching diplodocuses.

DID YOU SPOT?

The skull   2 yellow lizards   3 dragonflies

Stampede!

These little dinos will make a tasty snack for the ferocious allosauruses chasing them.
Can Max, Millie, and Mojo find a path through the crazy crowd?

70 million years ago

DID YOU SPOT?

The meteorite   2 broken dino eggs   3 dinosaur teeth

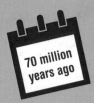

Dino Dodge

There are dinosaurs everywhere! Maybe they should visit another age where they're not so likely to end up as a dino's dinner. Help them tiptoe through the battling beasts.

70 million years ago

START

FINISH

DID YOU SPOT?

The dinosaur claw   The dinosaur egg   The dinosaur footprint

Mud Bath

Max, Millie, and Mojo have fallen into this muddy swamp, but they can see the time machine on the other side! Time to swim for it.

70 million years ago

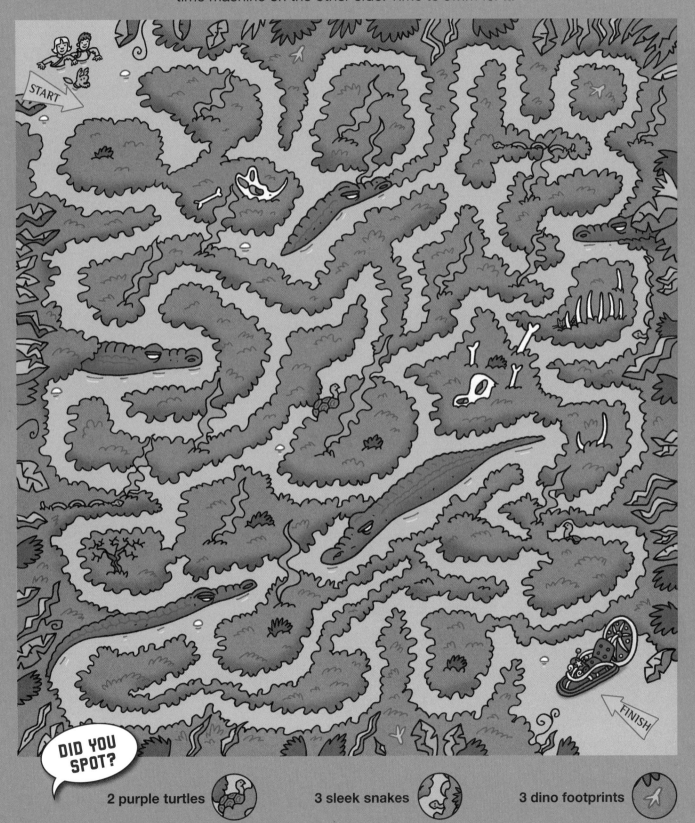

DID YOU SPOT?

2 purple turtles   3 sleek snakes   3 dino footprints

Mammoths on the March

The time machine has whisked our friends further forward in time to the Ice Age. Help them across the snow and through this huge herd of marching mammoths.

START

FINISH

DID YOU SPOT?

The smilodon   The woolly rhino   5 snowflakes

Painted Cave

Brrr, it's cold! The gang have climbed into a cave to get warm. Can you trace a path through the cave paintings to the entrance where the time machine is waiting?

20,000 years ago

DID YOU SPOT?

The strange statue

The paint pot

3 brushes

Standing Stones

This must be the Stone Age. And there are some Stone-Age people! Perhaps one of them can help. Can you pick a path through the giant monuments?

START

FINISH

DID YOU SPOT?

3 axes

4 arrowheads

4 rabbits

Contour Challenge

Mojo has run off and now he's stuck on the top of this burial mound.
Help him rejoin the gang at the bottom.

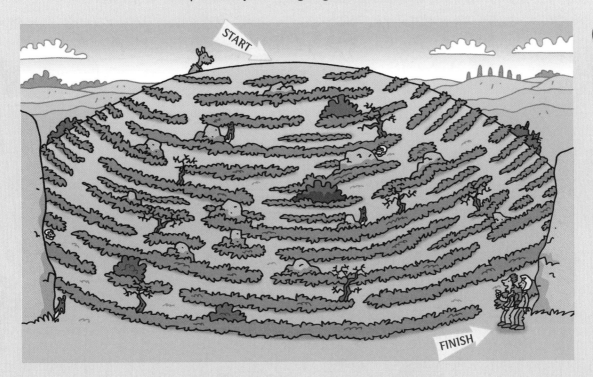

2 skulls

3 weasels

On the Farm

Max, Millie, and Mojo have arrived at a farm. The farmers think the village chief across the river might be able to help. Guide the gang through the field to the boat.

3 crows

3 baskets

Down the River

Help the gang paddle the canoe across the busy, fast-flowing river to the village.
Watch out for the jumping fish!

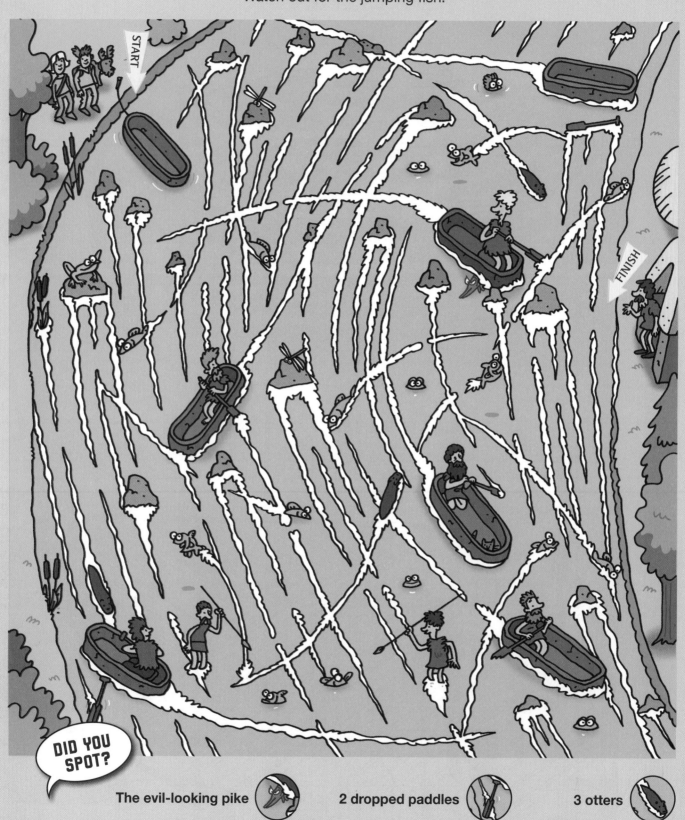

DID YOU SPOT?

The evil-looking pike   2 dropped paddles   3 otters

Village Life

Max, Millie, and Mojo need to find their way through the Stone Age huts to where the village chief is waiting for them.

DID YOU SPOT?

The cooking pot

The pig

3 stone axes

Chapter 3
Age of the Ancients

The village chief has given the gang a magic amulet. Maybe it will take them back to the present. They climb back into the time machine, give the amulet a rub, and adjust the controls. Where will they end up?

Land of the Pharaohs

This isn't the present! The gang have been whisked into the future, but only to the time of ancient Egypt. Help them climb the pyramid to see the pharaoh. Maybe he'll know what to do.

FINISH

START

DID YOU SPOT?

The sphinx

3 sinister birds

3 obelisks

The Future is Written

The pharaoh has told them to go inside the pyramid and look at these hieroglyphics. Wow!
The story seems to be about the gang. Can you get to the end and find out what's going to happen?

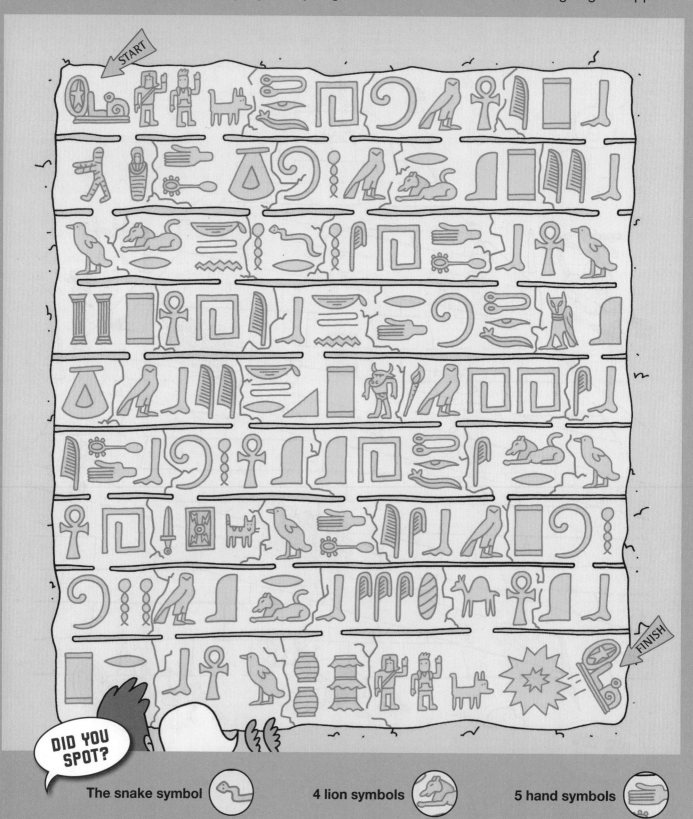

DID YOU SPOT?

The snake symbol   4 lion symbols   5 hand symbols

Oh Mummy!

The gang need to get back to the time machine, so they can travel to another age. But first they've got to make their way through this room full of dancing mummies.

The year 2000 bce

Going for Gold

The year 400 bce

The gang have gone forward in time to ancient Greece, but the time machine has gone missing! Help them run through these competitors at the Olympic Games so they can look for it.

START

FINISH

DID YOU SPOT?

The trumpet

The Olympic flame

4 discuses

28

The Temple of Zeus

It's a giant temple filled with statues. Our friends want to find the way to the mysterious door by the statue of Zeus, the leader of the Greek gods.

The year 400 bce

DID YOU SPOT?

The winged helmet   2 tridents   2 shields

Into the Labyrinth

The time machine was stolen by the minotaur, a scary monster that's half bull, half human. The gang will have to be careful finding their way through the labyrinth to get it back.

DID YOU SPOT?

The ball of string   2 swords   3 burning torches

30

On the March!

The gang have now landed in ancient Rome. They've decided to find the emperor to ask his advice. But first they need to weave their way through all these marching soldiers.

DID YOU SPOT?

The eagle standard

The catapult

3 plumed helmets

Roman Run

There's the emperor! But to reach him, the gang are going to have to tiptoe through all these fierce gladiators and animals fighting in the Colosseum.

DID YOU SPOT?

The lute The bag of coins 8 dropped shields

The Silk Road

The Roman emperor can't help them. He's told them to head down a long and winding path known as the Silk Road to China to find the emperor there.

The year 800

DID YOU SPOT?

The elephant   4 camels   5 silk moths

Lighting the Way

The gang have arrived in ancient China. Help them weave through the lanterns to where the Chinese emperor is waiting.

 **DID YOU SPOT?**

2 umbrellas

3 kites

 The year 800

Shadow Mojo

The emperor has taken them to see a shadow puppet show. And look, it's all about Mojo. Can he find a way through the Zodiac animals to get the bone?

 DID YOU SPOT?

The puppeteer's hand

The fan

34

Boom!

The emperor is holding a party for the gang with lots of fireworks. They've been fired up into the sky on a rocket. Guide them down to the time machine. Careful now!

DID YOU SPOT?

The pink and yellow rocket   **The panda**   **3 bats**

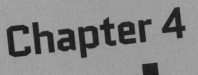

Chapter 4
Round the Castles

One of the fireworks exploded beneath the time machine and has sent the gang flying into the future. They've landed in the Middle Ages at the court of the English king, Henry VIII. He's promised to help the gang – but at a price. First, they'll have to travel around the medieval world, collecting as much treasure as they can for the greedy king.

Viking Raid

First stop is back to the age of the Vikings. These fearsome warriors from Scandinavia
have left some treasure behind for our friends. Help them find it.

DID YOU SPOT?

The trumpet **The helmet with the upside down horn** **4 seals**

The year 1100

Nimble Ninjas

Max, Millie, and Mojo have headed east to Japan where the emperor has given them lots of treasure. But now they'll have to choose the right route through the ninja warriors.

DID YOU SPOT?

The dropped sword   The bonsai tree   3 monkeys

Charge!

Our friends have gone looking for jewels in Central Asia, and now they need to get back to their time machine. But first they must cross the fierce, charging horseman of Genghis Khan.

The year
1200

DID YOU SPOT?

The helmet with two points

3 eagles

The blue flag

39

Through the Jets

After all that exercise, the gang need to cool off. And what better way than by dodging through the dancing fountains of Spain's Al-Hambra palace?

DID YOU SPOT?

4 butterflies

2 fish

The year
1400

Into (and out of) Africa

The gang have headed to sunny Africa to dry off. Make sure they don't take any wrong turns (and wake a sleeping lion) in the mighty fortress of Great Zimbabwe.

DID YOU SPOT?

2 sleeping lions

3 Zimbabwe birds

Fortress City

Our friends are at the crossroads of Europe and Asia in Constantinople, one of the most heavily defended cities in the world. A reward awaits them in the middle, if they can dodge the guards.

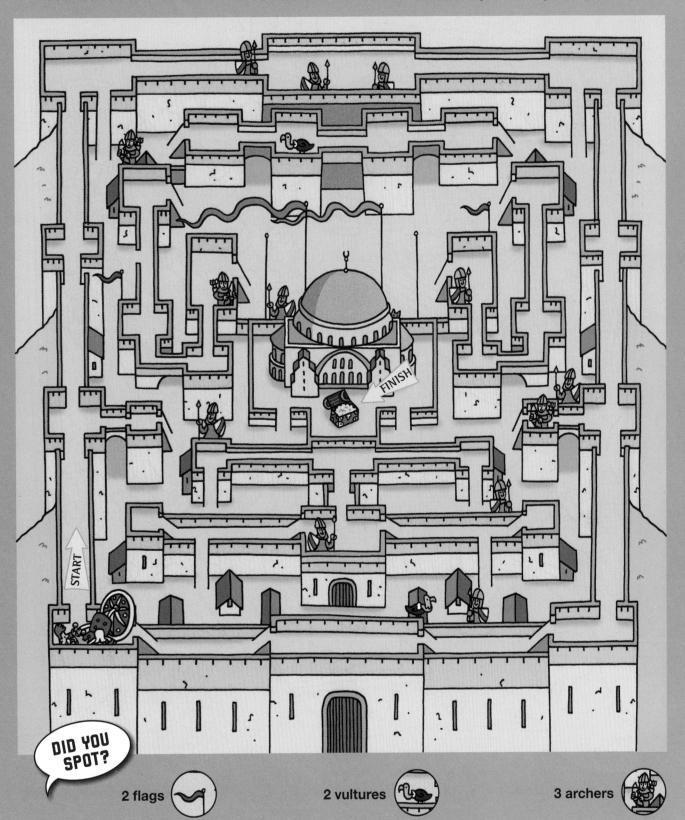

DID YOU SPOT?

2 flags   2 vultures   3 archers

Art Attack

On their way back to England, the gang have decided to stop off in Italy during the Renaissance.
They're going to get the famous artist Michelangelo to paint them a picture.

DID YOU SPOT?

The pot of paint   2 dropped chisels   3 dropped paintbrushes

Sent to the Tower

The final stop of the gang's Medieval World tour is the Tower of London.
Help them climb its walls to collect the treasure on the roof.

DID YOU SPOT?

2 polar bears   3 fearsome knights   5 ravens

43

Lance-A-Lot

Max, Millie, and Mojo are finally back at the court of Henry VIII where an exciting jousting tournament is taking place. The king should be delighted with all that treasure.

START

FINISH

DID YOU SPOT?

The dropped gauntlet

2 pet falcons

2 swords

Hampton Court Maze

What's this? Henry has hidden the time machine in the middle of his own maze.
Mojo has found it. Can Max and Millie get there too?

FINISH

START

DID YOU SPOT?

The bag of coins

2 crowns

3 rabbits

Chapter 5
The New World

To get to the present, the king thinks the gang should first head back into the past to find the most famous explorer of all time – Christopher Columbus. He was the first European to set eyes on the Americas – so if anyone will know how to get somewhere, it's surely him. But they'll have to find him first, and that means heading west to the New World.

Big Heads

The year 1492

The gang have arrived in what is now Mexico. These giant heads were carved thousands of years ago by the Olmecs, one of the first great civilizations of the Americas.

START

FINISH

DID YOU SPOT?

The jaguar

2 jade masks

4 monkeys

City of the Aztecs

The gang have made their way to Tenochtitlan, the capital city of the Aztecs. Guide them through the streets to the emperor. Maybe he'll know where Columbus is.

START

FINISH

DID YOU SPOT?

The calendar stone   2 eagles   3 snakes

The Ball Game

The emperor has challenged the gang to a friendly ball game. Our friends need to slam dunk a rubber ball in the stone ring before they can head on their way.

DID YOU SPOT?

The Armadillo

4 rubber balls

3 cacti

The Great Plains

Mojo's jumping skills helped them win the game, and now the gang are exploring North America. Maybe this Cheyenne chieftain will know where to find Columbus.

50

5 baby bison   **2 coyotes**   **3 cacti**

Totem Poles

The year
1492

In the far northwest of America, our friends have come across a thick forest filled with towering totem poles carved by Native Americans. But still no sign of Columbus.

DID YOU SPOT?

2 canoes   3 beavers   The puma

Inca Fortress

The gang have headed to South America to the Inca fortress of Machu Picchu. The emperor has
told our friends where to find Columbus – he's in the Caribbean. Now they must race back to the time machine.

START

FINISH

DID YOU SPOT?

The panpipe player   2 llamas   2 condors

All Aboard!

At last, the gang have found Columbus. Help them find their sea legs as they wriggle through the crew to the front of the boat.

The year 1492

DID YOU SPOT?

The map

3 seagulls

Lost at Sea

Oh dear. It seems that Columbus isn't such a great explorer after all. He's actually lost. Help him weave his way through the islands to the open sea.

The year 1492

DID YOU SPOT?

2 messages in bottles

4 flying fish

Chapter 6
Great Minds

Columbus couldn't help the gang get back to the present. So they're going to visit some of the greatest thinkers of the age to see if they know what to do. First stop is Renaissance Italy where they're hoping to meet the painter, inventor, scientist, and all-round clever-clogs, Leonardo da Vinci.

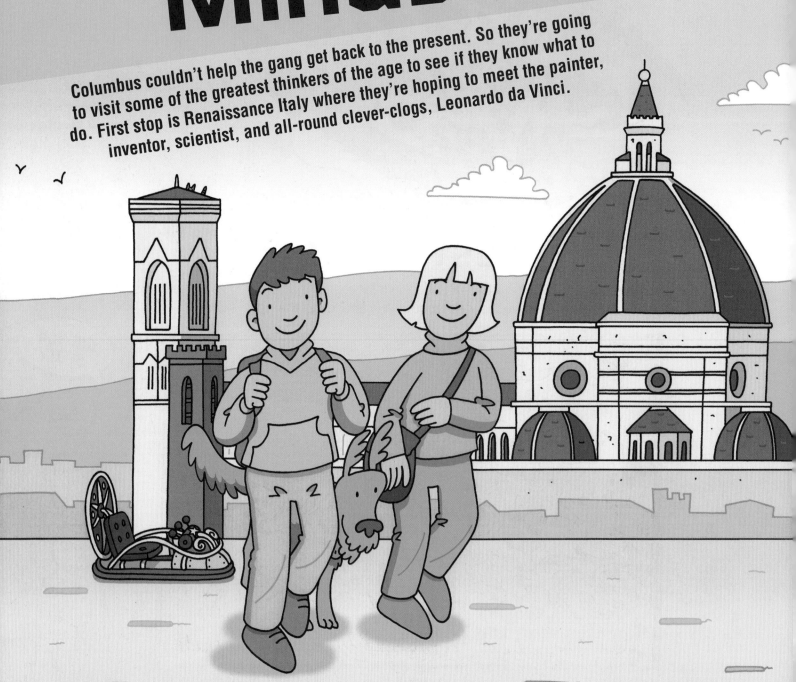

Ahead of his Time

Leonardo has invented many wonderful contraptions, including a tank, a helicopter, and a flying machine. Maybe he understands time machines too.

DID YOU SPOT?

The globe   The notebook   3 potion bottles

Lean on Me

No luck there, but who's that on top of the Leaning Tower of Pisa? It's the Italian astronomer, Galileo, one of the first men to look at the planets through a telescope.

DID YOU SPOT?

The spider   2 telescopes   5 pigeons

Take a Bow

They've drawn a blank in Italy, so it's time to tap some of England's great minds. Maybe William Shakespeare, the world famous playwright, can find the words to fix the time machine.

The picture of Queen Elizabeth I   **3 quill pens**   **3 candles**

57

The year
1700

Falling Down

Now they need to dodge the falling apples to find Sir Isaac Newton, one of the greatest scientists of all time. He discovered the laws of gravity – perhaps he knows the laws of time too.

58

The badger   **2 owls**   **3 field mice**

Listen to the Band

The great minds of England weren't much help, so Max, Millie, and Mojo have taken a trip to Austria for a little music, as played by the famous composer Wolfgang Amadeus Mozart.

DID YOU SPOT?

2 dropped wigs   3 music sheets   6 candlesticks

The Shocking Truth

The gang are back in the Americas. Help them through the lightning bolts to where the great US inventor, scientist, and politician Benjamin Franklin is conducting an electrical experiment.

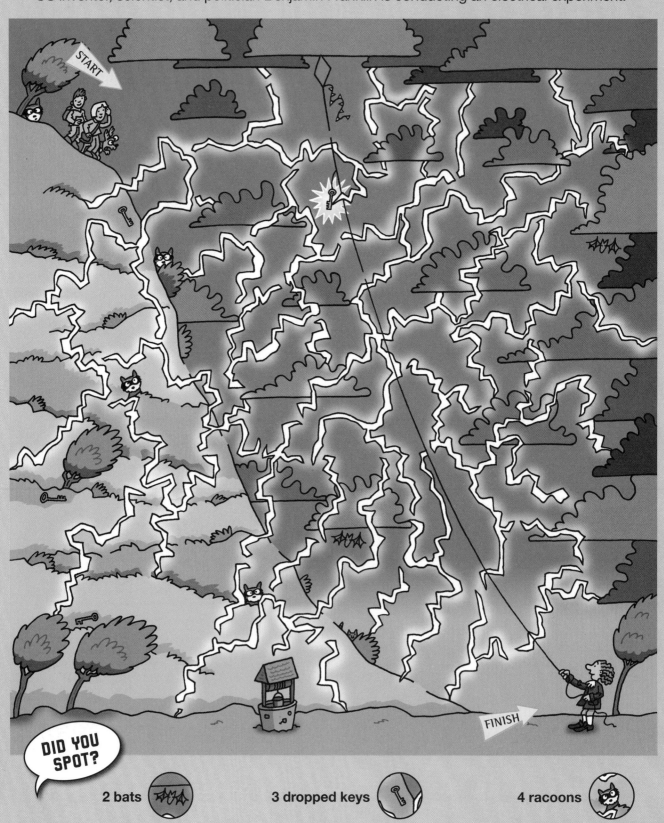

DID YOU SPOT?

2 bats   3 dropped keys   4 racoons

A Presidential Welcome

Franklin has sent them to find his friend, George Washington, the first President of the United States of America. Row them across the frozen river to where the president is waiting.

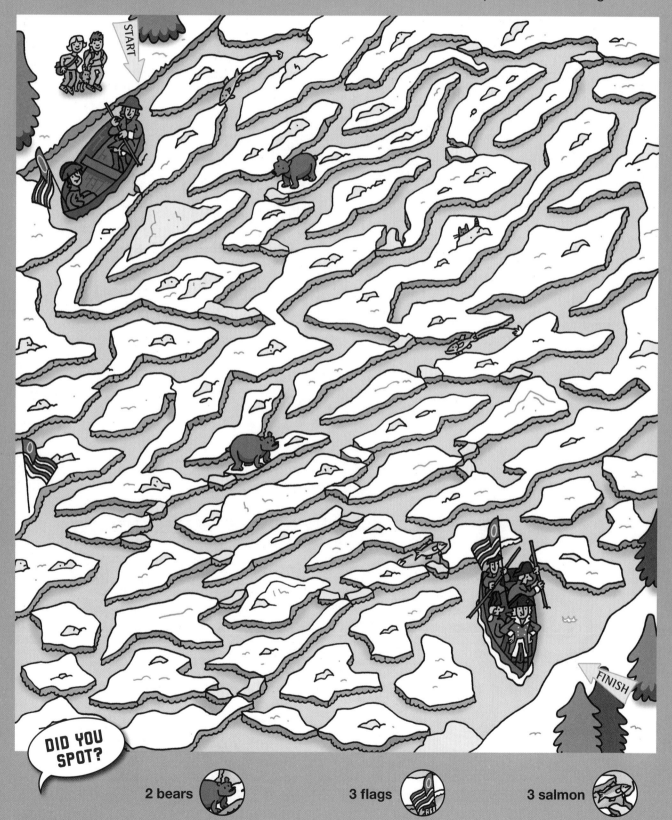

DID YOU SPOT?

2 bears   3 flags   3 salmon

A Trip to the Palace

The year 1789

Washington has sent them to France to see the wealthy king and queen, Louis XVI, and Marie Antoinette. Maybe the royals can pay for the gang to get back to the present.

DID YOU SPOT?

2 spiders

3 crowns

Revolution!

The year 1789

Oops! Looks like the royals will have to run for it. The poor people of France have started a revolution to overthrow the monarchy. Help the gang escape back to the time machine.

DID YOU SPOT?

The plate of cakes

3 pigeons

Don't get Blown Apart!

The year 1799

The gang are looking for Napoleon Bonaparte, the man who became leader of France after the Revolution. One of the greatest generals in history, he might have a strategy for getting home.

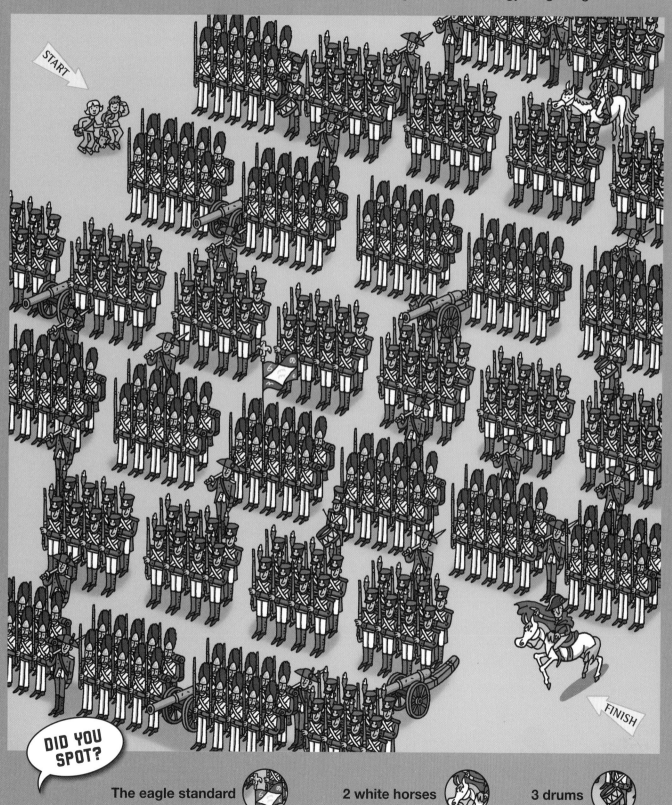

DID YOU SPOT?

The eagle standard   2 white horses   3 drums

Chapter 7
The Age of Machines

Napoleon has told them that he's an army man, not a scientist. They need to get in touch with some of the great inventors of the new industrial age. Perhaps the Montgolfier Brothers, the men who invented the hot-air balloon, can help. They've conquered the skies, so maybe they can conquer time, too.

Up in the Air

Help the Montgolfier brothers, Joseph and Jacques, carefully deliver Max, Millie, and Mojo back down to the time machine.

DID YOU SPOT?

The cow   2 rabbits   6 pigeons

Industrial Revolution

The brothers couldn't help, so the gang have travelled to Britain to find James Watt, the master of the new-fangled steam engine. Guide them through the smoking factory chimneys to his workshop.

DID YOU SPOT?

3 wheelbarrows   3 buckets   4 rats

Scaling the Steam Engine

There he is! Help our friends clamber up the enormous, whirring steam engine to where the great inventor is waiting.

The year 1800

FINISH

START

DID YOU SPOT?

2 pairs of pliers   2 hammers   4 spanners

The Crystal Palace

The year 1851

James has told them to head to the Crystal Palace where all the world's best inventors have gathered for an exhibition. Help them climb up its glass walls to meet Queen Victoria and Prince Albert.

DID YOU SPOT?

The dropped crown   The golden staff   3 spiders

Steaming Along

The queen has put them on a steam train with tickets to meet the most famous inventor of the Victorian age, Isambard Kingdom Brunel. But Mojo is stuck at the back. What should he do?

DID YOU SPOT?

2 cows

2 rabbits

Bridging the Gap

 The year 1855

Mojo has fallen behind again. Help him clamber down from one side of this suspension bridge to the other where Max and Millie are waiting.

DID YOU SPOT?

2 goats

4 seagulls

69

Ship Shape

Help the gang climb on board the 'SS Great Eastern', the biggest ship in the world, where its designer, Isambard Kingdom Brunel, has got some advice for them.

FINISH

START

DID YOU SPOT?

The stovepipe hat   4 mice   4 seagulls

Start Your Engines

Brunel has told them to find someone who knows about cars, not boats. So they're now in Germany to track down the pioneers of the motor car, Karl and Bertha Benz. There they are!

DID YOU SPOT?

The bicycle   2 spare tyres   3 dropped cranks

The year 1895

Let there be Light

Still looking for an answer, the gang have crossed the Atlantic Ocean to meet Thomas Edison, the inventor of the light bulb. Maybe he'll have a bright idea!

START

FINISH

DID YOU SPOT?

2 mice   3 moths   4 spiders

The Lightning Master

Edison has shown them where to find an even more talented scientist, a man who can actually control electricity, Nikola Tesla. Guide the gang to him through the giant sparks.

The year 1905

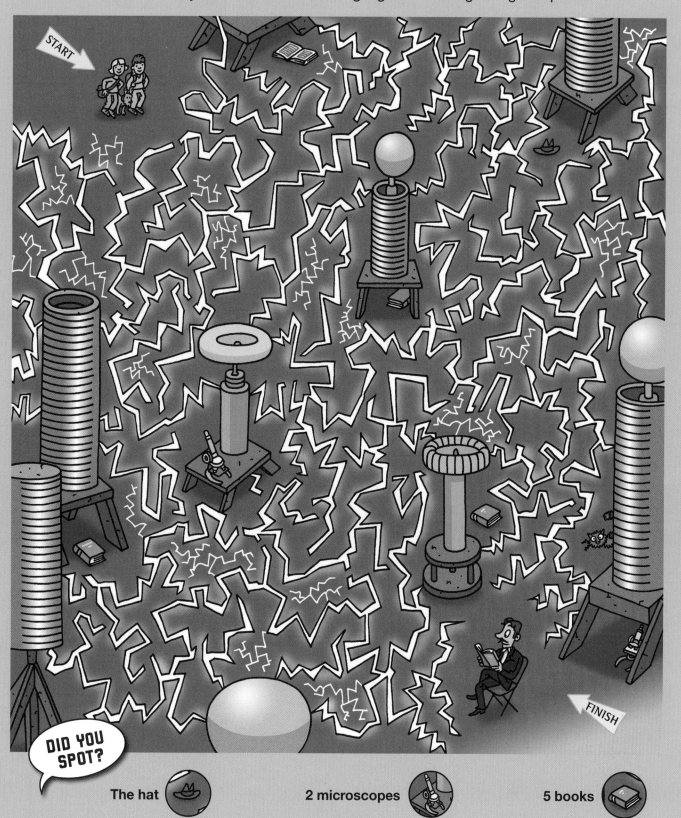

DID YOU SPOT?

The hat   2 microscopes   5 books

Chapter 8
Back to the Present

Even Nicola Tesla, the master of lightning, wasn't able to help them. But he's told them about a scientist who definitely can, the most famous scientist of all time – Albert Einstein. And Tesla has one more trick up his sleeve. He sends a powerful bolt of electricity towards the Time Machine. It buzzes and suddenly begins to hover – now the gang can fly!

Airship Odyssey

Max, Millie, and Mojo have taken to the skies on the search for Einstein. Help them weave and twist through these Zeppelins.

75

Plane Crazy

There's more air traffic for the gang to find a way through. Now the sky is filled with bi-planes. Guide them down to Wilbur and Orville Wright, the inventors of the plane.

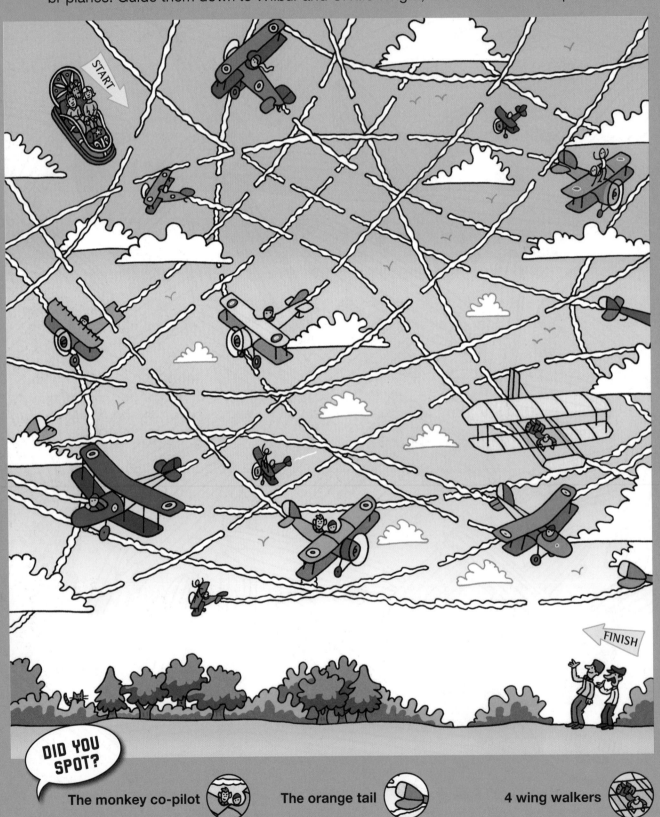

Early Whirly Birds

Looks like the Wright brothers have put the gang on the right path. Steer them up through these early helicopters to the great astronomer, Edwin Hubble. He'll know where Einstein is.

The year 1925

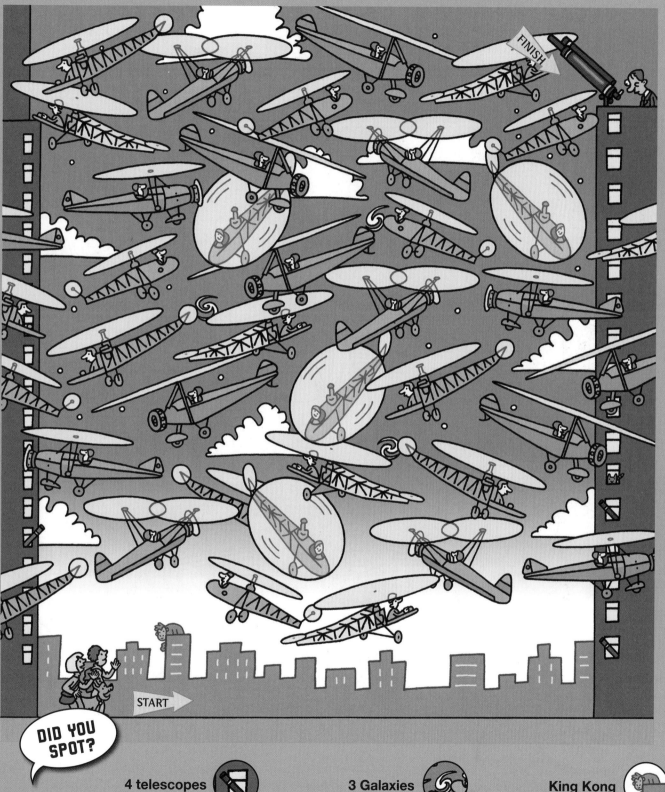

DID YOU SPOT?

4 telescopes   3 Galaxies   King Kong

I See (Through) You

Einstein is in the building, but first they need to pass through this science laboratory where Marie Curie is experimenting with radioactivity. Watch out for the X-Rays.

DID YOU SPOT?

2 petri dishes   3 dropped test tubes   3 pens

Easy Einstein

Professor Einstein has just finished giving a lecture. Help the gang through the audience to meet him.

DID YOU SPOT?

3 books

3 pens

Showing the Way

Einstein knows what to do! The gang must head to the Moon where there's a time portal that will take them back to the present. Help them plan their route.

DID YOU SPOT?

2 bats

2 owls

79

Race to the Moon

With their space helmets on, the gang are on their way to the Moon. But they must dodge all the super-speedy US and Soviet rockets that are trying to get there first.

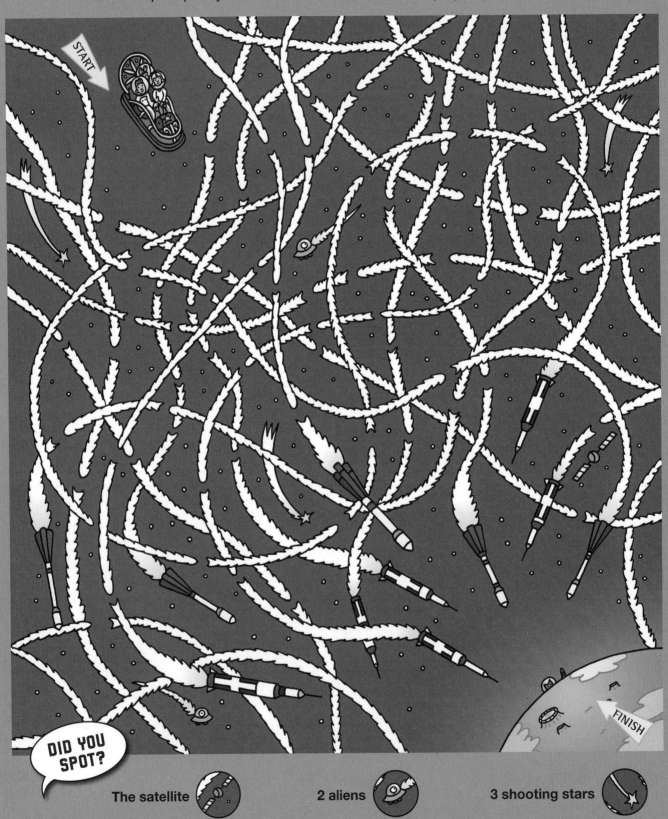

DID YOU SPOT?

The satellite

2 aliens

3 shooting stars

The Way Home

They've made it to the portal! Now they must be sure to pick the right path back to the museum. Choose carefully now!

The year 1965

DID YOU SPOT?

The dropped helmet · 2 meteorites · 2 Moon spiders

Back with a Bump

At last! It's good to be back. Now they need to get the time machine back in its box. Help them push it through some rather familiar looking exhibits.

START

FINISH

DID YOU SPOT?

A dinosaur tooth   2 quill pens   3 apples

Celebration Time!

Today

Time to go home. Max, Millie, and Mojo are going to put the time machine in a storeroom and out of harm's way. Guide them to the exit where they can enjoy a well-earned ice cream!

DID YOU SPOT?

The fire extinguisher   2 security guards   3 dropped ice cream cones

Answers

Museum Muddle

page 5

Medieval Madness!

page 6

Travels Through Time

page 7

The Time Machine

page 8

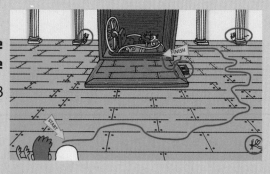

Taking Control!

page 8

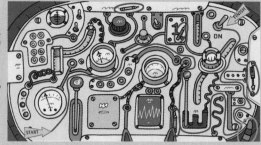

ime Tumble

page 9

Ferny Forest

page 13

Crash Landing

page 10

Grazing Giants

page 14

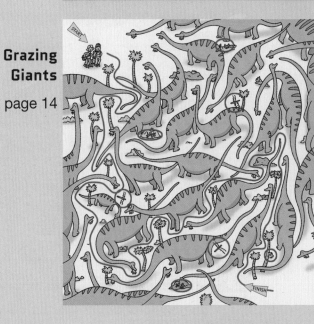

Future Fix

page 11

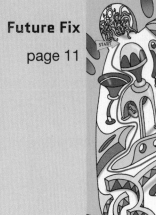

Stampede!

page 15

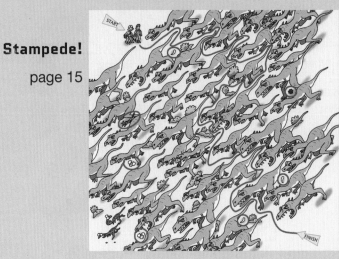

Dino Dodge

page 16

Painted Cave

page 19

Mud Bath

page 17

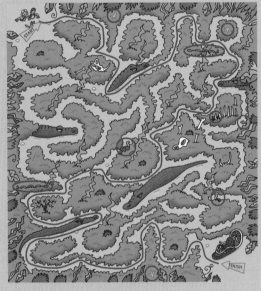

Standing Stones

page 20

Mammoths on the March

page 18

Contour Challenge

page 21

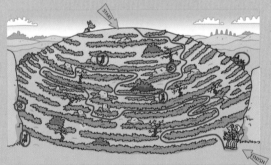

On the Farm

page 21

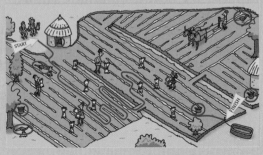

Down the River
page 22

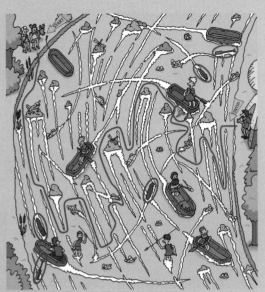

The Future is Written
page 26

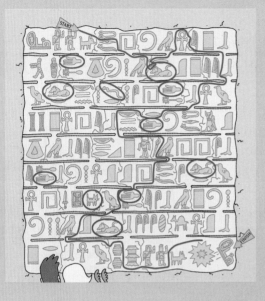

Village Life
page 23

Oh Mummy!
page 27

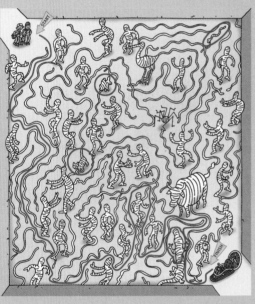

Land of the Pharaohs
page 25

Going for Gold
page 28

The Temple of Zeus

page 29

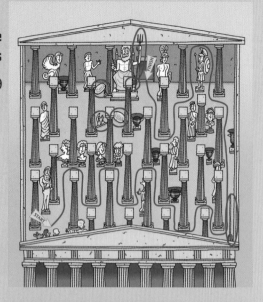

Roman Run

page 32

Into the Labyrinth

page 30

The Silk Road

page 33

On the March!

page 31

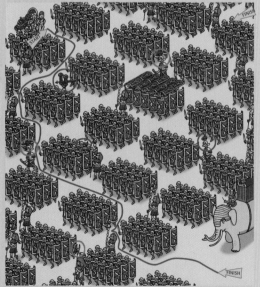

Lighting the Way

page 34

Shadow Mojo

page 34

Boom!

page 35

Charge!

page 39

Viking Raid

page 37

Through the Jets

page 40

Into (and out of) Africa

page 40

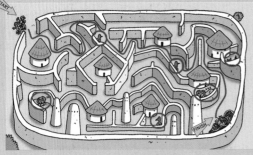

Nimble Ninjas

page 38

Fortress City

page 41

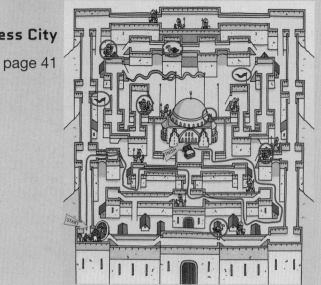

Lance-A-Lot

page 44

Art Attack

page 42

Hampton Court Maze

page 45

Sent to the Tower

page 43

Big Heads

page 47

City of the Aztecs
page 48

Totem Poles
page 51

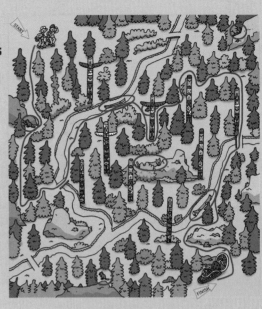

The Ball Game
page 49

Inca Fortress
page 52

The Great Plains
page 50

All Aboard!
page 53

Lost at Sea

page 53

Take a Bow

page 57

Ahead of his Time

page 55

Falling Down

page 58

Lean on Me

page 56

Listen to the Band

page 59

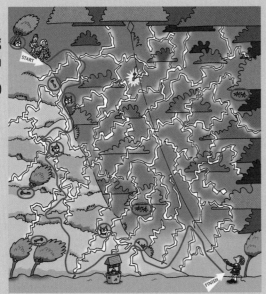

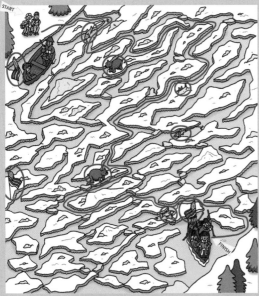

Industrial Revolution

page 66

Steaming Along

page 69

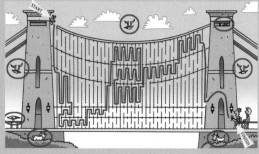

Bridging the Gap

page 69

Scaling the Steam Engine

page 67

Ship Shape

page 70

The Crystal Palace

page 68

Start your Engines

page 71

Let there be Light

page 72

Plane Crazy

page 76

The Lightning Master

page 73

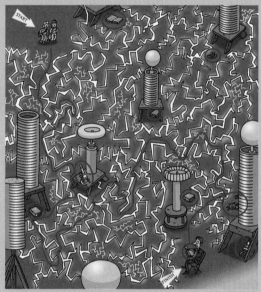

Early Whirly Birds

page 77

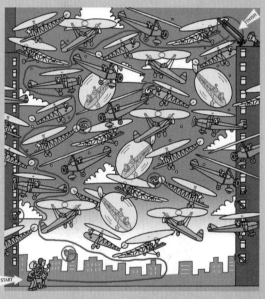

Airship Odyssey

page 75

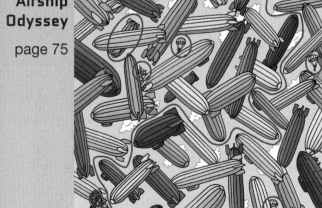

I See (Through) You

page 78

Easy Einstein

The Way Home

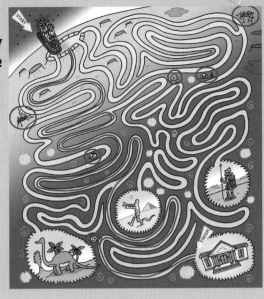

Showing the Way

Back with a Bump

Race to the Moon

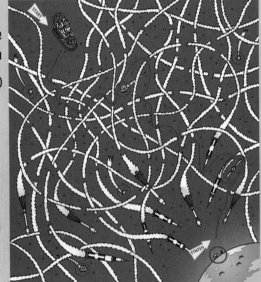

Celebration Time!